Canvas of a method of "de-radicalisation"
within a secular framework
that takes into account the belief itself.

Foreword

Saturday, Nov. 25, 2017: Egypt mourned 305 people, including 27 children, killed during the weekly prayer at the Al-Rawda mosque in Bir al-Abed, northeast of the country. And this is just one example among many: Muslims are the first victims of Islamic terrorism. And they are the first to be interested in what Western rulers call "de-radicalisation".

Some people think that DAESH's black flag is the plaything of foreign interests, but the fact remains that this flag is held by Muslims who believe in good faith that they not only can but must carry out an attack, invested with a mission of judging the world and establishing the reign of God on a land finally purified of the Antichrist.

The "Faith, Land, Mediation" Group deeply respects the just desire for the world to live according to the law of the Creator. The "Canvas of deradicalisation method" is addressed to the Muslim intelligence as a human intelligence wishing to correspond to its Creator. This is why the Framework chooses to begin by reading the daily prayer, and, from there, let the questions that rise in the heart and in the intelligence rise.

Here are some of these questions:

If God is the "Master of the Day of Judgement", who can claim that this "day" would come soon through a military victory or a political takeover? If God is the "Master", and if God is truly Allah, the Most Great, who can claim to judge and kill in His Name?

Associated with the idea of a judgment in the last days, where do Muslim ideas of an Antichrist? and a return of Christ come from?

Other questions deserve to be formulated, even without being able to answer them. What is behind the keen interest shown in Arab countries by Mel Gibson's film on the Passion of Christ? Could evil be defeated without killing "the wicked"? Is there an innocent blood that can defeat the power of Satan-Iblis? Isn't there a knot between these questions and the blood of the victim, or even that of the terrorist who sacrifices himself in the attack?

Caught up in the turmoil of wars, or simply in the turmoil of the suburbs, many Muslims suffer without being able to formulate these profound questions, which are questions of the meaning of life and death, questions of the future of life in society: questions of dignity and nobility, questions of man.

Introduction

In terms of "de-radicalisation", the remedies proposed by government initiatives have not borne the hoped-for fruit, as is now recognised. Various reasons have been put forward; they all revolve around the superficiality of the steps taken, which treat radical Islamist belief as a psychological or sociological phenomenon, without going into its very object.

While we are aware of the "evil" present in today's world dominated by money relations, we can think that there are real "good" answers other than Islamist radicalisation - and that this in turn expects other answers than hamsters and poetry (which has been tried in France on imprisoned Islamists!). Certain fundamental questions will have to be addressed, if only to understand the real mechanism that animates Islamist type belief and its radical intolerance.

Various definitions of "Islamism" have been given. For our part, we will not dwell on those which tend to reduce this phenomenon to this or that psycho- or socio-logical aspect, for example violence: with the exception of a few madmen, no Islamist ever exalts violence for its own sake. Islamism is first of all a certain vision of the world, a world from which evil can - and therefore must - be eradicated. This simple idea has an equally simple consequence, as the saying goes: *you can't make an omelette without*

5

breaking eggs. If imposing Sharia law is to lead to a better world, then those who oppose it must be discriminated against and subjected (or even eliminated). Such an idea, which is a form of hope, is called "messianism" - and Islamism is not the only form, although it can be seen that it is in almost all civil societies in the world today that Islamist groups are developing. France is by no means a special case.

The basic problem is therefore not only the *means used by the* Islamists (propaganda, pressure, terrorism...) but also, and even more so, the *goals* pursued, which are always political but which are in line with what they believe to be a better world - we can see why many are ready to sacrifice their lives (and those of many others).

The *state of play leads* to one final question: is the aim pursued by those in charge really to "deradicalize" or to pretend? We will assume the first hypothesis, knowing that Islamists, from the Muslim Brotherhood (1923) to all those of today, have not failed to be used in geo-political strategy games. Our perspective will consist in contributing rationally to "deradicalize", by giving the means to address even and above all the most fanatical, provided they are capable of a minimum of thought. We need to enter into this thinking, where belief, linked to affectivity, holds a dominant place.

Sketch of a new method

In a country that respects human dignity, the method of "de-radicalisation" proposed here calls for a certain awareness. A sense of progressiveness and dialogue will be necessary on the part of supervisors, as well as an understanding of the final perspective of this dialogue, which can only be achieved gently but with conviction. The common thread: we will try to follow step by step the prayer verses that all Muslims know by heart, the Fâtiḥah - which will define the seven points of the first and essential part.

Then, in a short second part, it will remain to look at historical perspectives turned less towards the past than towards the future.

Indeed, "deradicalising" necessarily means achieving a certain "working together", which is much richer (and more realistic) than "living together". Indeed, what unites people is not simply being neighbours - this would often rather be an opportunity for war - but having common objectives and means of action. It is the awareness of having common interests that unites: it is a question of working together beyond communitarianism, for the good of civil society, for the good of families and for the good of our children, but realism consists in seeing that what unites is also to oppose together what threatens these goods. In this sense, de-radicalisation can and must go so far as to open up prospects for civil understanding.

I - Asking the problems: read Sura Al Fâtiḥah

Beginning with a sura as familiar and significant as Sura 1 opens an interesting path, verse after verse. Here is the text in a good translation:

1. In the name of God-Allah, Most Gracious, Most Merciful.

2. Praise be to God-Allah, Lord of the universe.

3. The Merciful, the Merciful,

4. Master of Judgment Day.

5. It is You whom we adore, You whom we implore for help.

6. Guide us on the right path,

7. The way of those whom Thou hast filled with favour, not of those who have incurred Thy wrath, nor of those who have gone astray.

1. Allah-God and Mercy

Bi-smi Llāh[i] r-raḥmān[i] r-raḥīm[i]

In the name of Allah,
the Merciful, the Compassionate

The word "Allah"

Contrary to popular belief, the word "Allah" does not belong to Islam per se; this is how God has always been referred to in Arabic, especially among Arab Christians. "Allah" or its Hebrew or Aramaic equivalents, Elohim or Alaha, simply means "God", the God who created everything. In fact, all these words are plurals, as Arab grammarians know about "Allah".

What could be higher or greater than God? Money? In a few hours, money can lose much of its value?

It should be noted that, from a historical point of view, there are Arabic names such as 'Abdallah, i.e. *servant of Allah, which were* used by Christian Arabs long before Islam. On the other hand, the name Muḥammad does not appear, as Islamic traditions attribute other names to the official founder of Islam: this suggests that he was the first to bear the name Muḥammad, which must have been a title or nickname given to him.

Both terms *raḥmān and raḥīm*

In verse 1, a particularly important word appears in two very close forms, *raḥmān / raḥīm,* which correspond roughly to *merciful / merciful.* The God who is merciful (raḥmān) - i.e. who is moved and desires the good of mankind - is merciful in Himself (raḥīm). This is logical: would God even once do something contrary to what He Himself is?

Here again, it is vital to awaken the mind to religious words. That alone is a huge step. At least it becomes possible to talk to each other, while realising that the formula: "God is merciful" does not necessarily mean the same thing to everyone.

Indeed, from other religious perspectives, it means that God really "bears" the bad, He does not condemn anyone: those who are "condemned" are not "condemned" by God but by their irrevocable will to do evil. We can say then that God is merciful not only to a particular group, but to every human being. For this is the question: if God is said to want the good of mankind throughout the ages, is it *all* mankind or just *some of* them?

Besides, *in Himself*, can God want good for some and bad for others? How can we explain that God can want bad? Is there a contradiction in Him, especially in the face of Satan-Iblis, who wants all possible evil for mankind? Would Satan be a servant of God according to God's will, doing evil? But then, what real difference would there be between a God who wants evil and Satan who does it?

It is important to address these questions fairly quickly, but without answering them: the important thing is to ask them, leaving everyone time to face them. They are crucial, perfectly logical and rational. Moreover, it would be unacceptable for a narrow and ideological secularism to prevent us from asking them: we might as well renounce all "deradicalisation".

Nevertheless, this is what happens objectively when judges (and previously the media) systematically qualify the perpetrators of attacks as "unbalanced": is this not a flight from the real issues? At the same time, it must be recognised that the idea of a God who wills good for some and evil for others is a source of psychological disorder. For then, am I among those to whom God wills good, or the opposite - will He send me to hell? Am I, in the image of that God, on earth to do good to some and harm to others? It is not by sending terrorists to psychiatry that we will help them to get out of this Islamist debate, even if schizophrenic tendencies can easily be detected.

2. Desire for the "God of the universe".

al-ḥamd^u li-Llāhⁱ rabbⁱ l-'ālamīn^a

Praise to God-Allah, Lord of the universe

Here again, you have to think and exchange, because the sentence is not that simple. Fâtiḥa awakens piety by directing the love and desire of the soul towards God, this is the meaning of the word "ḥamd" which means "praise" in Arabic, and "desire" in the Bible, i.e. in Hebrew and Aramaic. The verse invites to love God, which means that all people are made to know and praise God, to love and desire Him, to find their joy in Him and to place Him at the top of all the desires of their lives, He the Lord of the universe. Rationally, we deduce that:

-1- A certain "rank" must be assigned to desires, from the lowest that are unworthy of human beings to the highest that are turned towards God. All religious consciousness implies this perspective - clearly, it is not the one advocated in the dominant culture, whose "values" are sex, money and power. Islamism is the opposite of this culture. However, it should be noted that things are not as clear-cut. Didn't Daesh promise his activists to enjoy sex, money and power, precisely? Didn't he rely on certain traditions that promise this for this land and as retribution for the Hereafter? Didn't these traditions themselves rely on certain passages of the Koranic text taken literally?

Therefore, what right do we have to reproach others for

what we ourselves advocate?

And what should we think of a discourse that serves as a justification for enjoying sex, money and power in place of others?

The fundamental question here is this: "Is my desire true or is it something else? »

-2- Placing God above everything (sex, money, power) is totally legitimate if we believe that every man is capable of orienting himself towards God, and therefore that we do not have to pose as a priori judges of others. Consequently, one will consider that every man deserves respect a priori.

Indeed, God is said to be *rabb l-ʿālamīn which* can be translated as "Lord of the ages" as well as "of the universe" (literally: of the worlds). He has time. Why would He delegate to men to punish in His place by killing? Here it is assumed that everything is written in advance, and, moreover, that it is possible to know who God intends to punish or not, so that it can be done in advance and in His place. But is this the case? And besides, if everything is written in advance in a closed program, does it still make sense to do anything?

And who can claim to know such a divine programme, and to know who is destined for Heaven or Hell? It is in this sense that a fatwa, issued in Saudi Arabia a few years ago but forgotten, indicates that, to punish the unbelievers, it is necessary to wait until the last day of their life: it is indeed possible that they turn to God at some point in

14

their life, even at the last. Of course, this is an indirect way of saying that one should never take the life of a creature that could still turn to God.

Besides, if we do it anyway, don't we risk being in opposition to God? And, in fact, do we not thus arrogate to ourselves a prerogative of judgement that belongs to Him alone? And does God so despise human life?

And if one wants to "eradicate evil from the world", shouldn't one first redirect one's own desires?

These questions are numerous. As mentioned above, the current aim is not to answer them but to raise them. Together. And as rationally as possible.

In passing, let us note the risk of schizophrenia that exists between, on the one hand, dreaming of satisfying desires for sex, money and power and, on the other hand, praising Allah, i.e. placing Him higher than these human (often infra-human) desires. And what about frustrations! For all that, it would be very dangerous to deny a priori that the perpetrator of an attack is sane. One can be disturbed and very conscious of one's actions...

3. An emphasis on God's mercy

Ar-raḥmān[i] r-raḥīm[i]

the Merciful, the Compassionate

Verse 3 takes up what is already said in verse 1: it is therefore a capital lesson. Why is it so?

Fatiḥa insists on *mercy*.

In Arabic, the root of the word, "rḥm", as in other Semitic languages, refers to the womb, the insides of the woman, the uterus.

We are talking about a God who is a God of Life: He gives life, and He wants to maintain it and make it grow, for a community and for each person in particular.

We must not hide the difficulty that arises here. The image presented in the "Life of the Prophet" (*Sira an-nabawyya*), which Ibn Hišâm published two centuries after the beginnings of Islam, or in the collections of ḥadith-s, does not correspond at all to the meaning of the word *mercy* attributed to God. One only has to look at the list of murders and tricks that are on loan at Muḥammad (all this can easily be found on the web). But is this list true? What is a book written two centuries after the supposed facts worth? Wasn't it in the interest of the Caliphs of that time to portray a model that served their own interests, especially in order to justify their own oppressive, so often murderous system?

This vital question is also a logical one. The qualification of *raḥīm* given to God indicates that He is merciful *in Himself* (or *very merciful*). The basmallah, or verse 1, already said this. If God is merciful *in Himself*, can He be merciful only in His own time, without denying Himself? Is it possible for some to be merciful at times and for others to be merciful at other times? In this case, shouldn't the text of the basmallah say: "In the name of Allah, the Merciful, the Non-Merciful" (*ar-raḥmān wa la r-raḥīm*)? If we do not believe that God is *raḥīm*, *should* we not stop saying it in the basmallah?

These are questions to be raised, and they have nothing that would offend God-Allah.

And if God is merciful to the world, we can hope that this is what the demonstrators have in mind when they cry "Islam is the solution". But where do we see this "solution"? In Medina, at the time of the "Prophet"? The *Sira* and later sources do not give a heavenly image of this period, far from it. Even supposing it was Paradise, why did it cease? Why did the Islamists never manage to rebuild it?

Perhaps it belongs less to the past than to the future - like the fatwa that invited to wait for the last day of the miscreant. But on what condition?

Verse 4 gives the answer to this very question.

4. A Judgement to come

Mālik yawm[i] d-dīn[i]
Master of the Day of Judgment

The words

For the man who loves God, the "Day of Judgement" raises an immense hope: God will finally receive what is due to Him, and God's will will be done on earth - a will of life since God is *raḥîm*.

But what "Judgement" are we talking about exactly?

The word spontaneously brings to mind the judgment by which each man passes into eternity, with, afterwards, paradise for some (immediately or after a delay) and hell for others. This is why this verse is sometimes translated as "Master of the Day of Judgment". But the word "*dīn*" radically means "judgment". By extension in Arabic, it has also taken on the meaning of "religion", in the sense of "what is due to God".

This being so, the expression "Judgement Day" has a very precise, proper meaning, which is collective and not individual. It can already be found in the Gospels, as well as in religious texts both after and before Islam (Targums, various apocryphal texts, etc.). The word "Day" is as important as the word "Judgement". Which Day is it?

In these writings they speak of the judgment of men - of those who "on that Day" will be on earth. By this Judgment, in one way or another, the earth will have to be purified of those who have devoted themselves to evil. In practice, this means: from those who have dedicated themselves to the anti-Messiah (or *Antichrist*) of which Islamic traditions speak, although they differ in their description of these events. But all of them evoke a re-descent of the Messiah-Jesus (from Heaven).

It is important to emphasise that the world that is to result will not be the fruit of a jihad but radically that of God's intervention. So what sense does it make to think of playing the universal vigilante right now? Who would be "pure" or "just" enough to have the right to do so? And in relation to whom, and how?

These are the questions that arise.

Who will judge who and how?

• Can a man who has court cases judge other people's cases well? It is doubtful. If God is by definition the One **who judges**, He must have nothing to reproach Himself with – or, to put it another way: if God has the right to judge, it is because He is truly and uniquely a God of Life. If He were a God who also wants the death of those who do not please Him, any just man could stand up against Him and accuse Him (for this reason, there are Muslims today who call themselves atheists). Rationally, the possibility of Hell is not admissible here as an objection, at least not against a God who does not want evil and who is not responsible for the choice that every man is called to make.

• As for the subjects of the Judgement (= **who will be judged**), they must be the men who will be on earth on that Day. Some traditions want to associate those who have died before, but it is in another capacity that they would be concerned, since they have already passed through the judgment at their death (death being a passage). There is no difficulty here.

• On the other hand, the question of **how** the Judgement will be made is one of them. What Islamic commentators are saying is that Jesus (called '*Issa in* the Koran because of the inversion of two consonants), returning from Heaven, will have a great role to play. On earth, and even in a specific place. According to Christian writings, he ascended to Heaven from the Mount of Olives (opposite the esplanade of the mosques in Jerusalem): this is therefore the first place where Islamic traditions brought him down, but they later placed his descent on a minaret of the Umayyad Mosque in Damascus. This opinion, which is now in the majority, poses some difficulties because, having to go to the Temple Esplanade (Al-Quds) in Jerusalem, he would still have 160 km to walk, and he would have to cross a border which is closed - except for the jihadists who come and go in Israel, according to the many testimonies the press has been led to talk about. Moreover, the Golden Gate through which he would have to pass to get onto the esplanade is worse than closed: walled. And the double staircase behind it is backfilled. How is the Messiah going to do it?

Wouldn't it be easier for him to go elsewhere than to Jerusalem for the Judgement? The question is absurd, except that in a small village in northern Syria called Dabiq, an ancient tradition brought to light by Daesh places the great final battle between the forces of Good and Evil [1] . It has not been told to the jihadists indoctrinated in Europe and who went to Syria to be killed that it is there that the Messiah-Jesus would take the head of the armies and kill the Antichrist and his followers; yet it is more feasible to go from Damascus to Dabiq than to Jerusalem. Daesh's manipulators didn't think of this - nobody is perfect.

In any case, the figure of a Jesus superman coming to annihilate the Antichrist in Jerusalem and to lead exterminating armies there deserves to be mentioned. Where does such a story of material return and judgement come from[2]? It is not invented, and if it comes from somewhere, it is not as *such* from Christian traditions or texts (which present things differently).

Furthermore, assuming that the Judgement were to take place in this way, what would it lead to next? What better

---

[1] Hence the title of Daesh's multilingual monthly magazine - "the Islamic State of the Levant": *Dabiq*.

[2] According to historical research, Muḥammad would have announced the Day of Judgement, and especially the imminent descent of Jesus ('Issa) to earth.

world could come out of it? Under what conditions could the world be better?

In short, that's a lot of questions ...

Once again, the important thing is not to answer the questions but to be able to ask them together and rationally.

5. To worship and implore God?

^{iyyāka} na'budu wa-^{'iyyāka nasta'īnu}

It is You whom we adore,
You whom we implore for help.

In Arabic, the '*abd* is both a servant and a slave, and the verb '*abada* used in verse 5 refers to God: to *worship* Him. This verse also teaches us to *implore Him*. The two actions go together - at least that is clearly what the verse says. However, we may ask ourselves: why implore the God we adore if He has no intention of intervening on our behalf, if He is infinitely far from mankind?

But if we believe otherwise, a problem arises. If He cares about me, don't I risk a lot? If He is the Author of both good and evil - as we hear Him say in the name of His Almighty Power - it is perhaps better that I pass unnoticed and do not open my mouth to implore His help. For have I done Ramadan well? What does He require of me for me to be accepted, He who says: "God loves those who *go so far as to kill* (*qâtala*) in His way (i.e. for Him)" (Qur'an 61, 4)?

Should we therefore implore God or not? This verse 5 is not obvious at all.

Moreover, we see a relationship between "You" (God) and "us". Even if "we" are said to be Muslims, what real relationship can we have with a God who commands and acts totally in all things and in all people? What room is left for my personal responsibility? And why should there still be a Judgement if nothing deserves to be judged? Is there a "You" (God) in front of a "We"?

Or should I think that I am irresponsible? When I do evil, is it not God's fault ("It is not you who killed them, but God who killed them" - Koran 8:17)? Moreover, am I not pure and innocent by the fact that I am a Muslim, even if I do all possible evil? And in Heaven, will there be plenty of people who have committed atrocities but who are Muslims, while the good and just who are not Muslims will be in Hell?

Curiously, the Islamist discourse tells me that I am responsible, responsible for the spread of Islam. But what kind of Islam should I be a *mukallaf*, a militant? That of the Wahhabites? That of Indonesia, which is quite open (if we omit the genocide committed in East Timor in 1975)? Yet another one?

Besides, why would God need me if He is Almighty?

We can see that, whatever the aspect of things, logic comes up against a problem: is there a "We" in front of a "You" who is God?

A fundamental question arises: does the "face-to-face" with God that the Bible speaks of make sense, or do I not really exist face to face with God?

6. The right path

Ihdinā ṣ-ṣirāṭa l-mustaqīma /
Guide us on the right path

What is the "straight path"? If we say: "Guide us on the right path", we assume that there is another path, the wrong path. According to the last verse, which is affixed to the word "path" like a kind of gloss, there is more than one wrong path, there are even two, as we shall see: the path of the Jews and the path of the Christians. But why only two? Logically, this final verse should also have said something about Buddhists, Hindus and other groups.

In short, one may simply wonder whether the expression "the right way" originally referred to the very classical doctrine of the "two ways" (or "ways"), the right way and the wrong way.

The pre-Islamic doctrine of the "two ways".

In the Bible, in Psalm 27, we find the words of Fâtiḥah: "Teach me, O Lord, your way, guide me in the right *path*". The Hebrew has the word "*halakha*" from a Hebrew root which means to *walk,* to indicate a certain way of commenting on the Torah. The idea of "the straight path" comes from the fact that the Covenant, sealed by the Law, leads to life and happiness; disobeying it leads to death and misfortune (Deuteronomy 30:15-18). Here we have no division of humanity between the good and the wicked, but the fact that each is placed before two paths, one good and the other bad.

And when we read in Psalm 1:6: "The Lord knows the way of the righteous, but the way of the ungodly is lost", we should not read there either an opposition between the righteous and the wicked, but between the way of the righteous and the way of the wicked. Indeed, it is also written that a righteous man can become evil, and in that case his righteousness will not be remembered - the reverse is also true: "As for the wicked, if he renounces all the sins he has committed, observes all my laws and practises law and justice, he will live, he will not die. All the crimes he has committed will not be remembered; he will live because of the righteousness he has done" (Ezekiel 18:21-22).

Similar themes can be found in the Gospel[3].

It is important to perceive that in all these texts, the idea of "right of way" does not imply a partition of humanity between those who would be predestined for heaven and those who would be predestined for hell, nor between

---

[3] For example Matthew 7:13-14: "Wide is the gate, spacious is the way that leads to perdition, and many enter by it. But narrow is the gate, narrow is the way that leads to life, and there are few who find it". Christian writings from the 2nd century also present such a theme: the *Didachè*, the *Doctrina apostolorum,* the *Syriac Didascalia of the Twelve Apostles,* etc. Some Buddhist texts can be found that resemble these texts, but they are difficult to date (they seem to be much later).

those, the good ones, who would have the mission to kill the others, the bad ones. Neither does it imply a division of humanity between those who would be predestined for heaven and those who would be predestined for hell, nor between those who would be good and who would have the mission of killing others, the bad ones. Nor does it imply that there are two paths (each of which is the responsibility of a teaching and an authority: the path of light and the path of darkness*)*. Great is the difference between these two paths. In fact, the angels of God who give light are appointed to the one, and the angels of Satan to the other. One is Lord from eternity to eternity, the other is prince of the present age of iniquity" (§ 18-21).

Also in the second century, Hermas speaks of the crooked way, the way of darkness, saying that it is fatal for those who take it: "Trust in the righteous, but not in the unjust; for righteousness follows a **straight way,** injustice a crooked way. Therefore follow the straight and united way, and leave the crooked way. The **crooked way** is not straight, but impassable, full of obstacles, rocky, thorny. It is fatal to those who take it. But those who take the straight path walk on a smooth and unobstructed ground, for it is neither rocky nor thorny. So you see that it is more advantageous to take it" (*The Shepherd of* Hermas 35, 2-4). This teaching applies to the collective as well as to the individual: groups, communities or nations that follow the evil path will also have to regret it.

However, in some post-Christian texts, the idea of "two paths" sometimes seems to take a sociological turn, as if they could be two human groups opposed to each other. In the *Rule of the Community* found in a cave near the Dead Sea, we read: "The sons of justice ... walk in ways of light; ... the sons of perversion walk in ways of darkness" (3, 20-21). These are traditions with sectarian tendencies, likely to nourish a temptation of suprematism and intolerance.

Bad means but good end?

Despite their differences, none of these texts would have said that doing wrong could be part of the right path under the pretext of pursuing a good objective. This is a serious and difficult issue. In view of a good to be achieved - real or supposed - can I commit evil? Does the end justify the means, as we sometimes hear people say?

When we talk about the "straight path", we are supposed to know where it leads. One can believe in good faith that the goal of the path is good when it is not, and in any case this is debatable. And even if the goal seems good, are all the means that seem to achieve it good for all that? That makes two questions.

-1- Let's first look at the means. According to current US military doctrine, it is acceptable to kill up to ten civilians to eliminate a single jihadist. Isn't that disgusting? Wahhabi preachers teach that it is permissible and even useful to lie for the cause of Islam - this is the famous *taqqiya*, which Shiite preachers also teach. Is all this the right way?

-2- Let us now consider the "end" of the path, i.e. the goal sought - or what is presented as such, because there are many manipulations. Who would be against a better and fairer world? Everyone dreams of an ideal society to build. This dream stirs something very deep in the human heart and mind. The history of Europe shows that this dream has been used many times to motivate people in internal or world wars, and the history of Islam shows it too. Where is the mistake?

During Islamist demonstrations in Britain, one could see placards saying: "Islam is the solution". This means: "Just apply Sharia law to the world and you will have an ideal world - as God wants it". This theme is central to the thinking of the Muslim Brotherhood and the Taliban, but do we know enough that the former organised themselves almost a century ago thanks to MI5, the British secret service (so that they could exalt Arab Islam against the Turks), and that the latter were founded in Afghanistan by the CIA, the US secret service? Can an ideal or even simply better world emerge from these manipulations?

Let's ask the question differently. In Syria, against whom are the jihadists fighting? Against the predators of this world, against corruption, against the Antichrist? No, against a Sunni state that makes various Muslim groups coexist, and also populations other than Muslims (it's secularism in the Syrian style). Who pays them? In arms alone, several billion dollars have been invested by powers that want the Syrian state to disappear. Since 2017, the involvement of the State of Israel in the conflict has been growing stronger and stronger, and it is no longer forbidden to say that it exists (since the beginning, as we know today). This conflict will have caused almost two hundred thousand deaths and millions of refugees, both inside and outside the country. The UN estimates the damage suffered by the country at 235 billion dollars. For the benefit of those who fight the Islamists, if not those who pay them or even occupy part of the territory with their own army (2018)?

In the light of these realities, the path of the Islamists appears to be contrary to the "right path"; it is bad from the point of view of both the objectives and the means employed. It should even be pointed out that :
- A straight path *both* pursues a good goal *and* uses good means;
- if a path pursues bad goals, it is bad, even if it uses some acceptable means;
- and if a path aims at a good goal but uses bad means, it is also bad.

Trap and handling

At the end of the day, is it not taking God's place to want to divide humans between a camp of the good (to which one obviously belongs) and a camp of the bad? The trap is enormous. A doctrine that cuts humanity in two is a doctrine of hatred. President Bush has proposed such a doctrine, speaking of the "axis of Good" versus the "axis of Evil". But what else do Salafist preachers do when they teach to hate Jews and Christians? They too cut the world in two. On the other side, Egyptian President El-Sissi has asked - or pretends to ask - Cairo's Al-Azhar University to withdraw the books and courses that give such teaching... which can also be heard on state television! How can we fail to see that it is not God who is behind this trap of hatred, but sordid interests?

For those who push to hate to the point of killing, lying and raping, those who have been paid to convince young people to go and be killed in Syria, in their sermons at the mosque, obey global projects which are beyond us - and which are sometimes described as projects of "controlled chaos"[4].

---

[4] On traduit ainsi des expressions anglaises telles que " global chaos " ou " controlled / planned chaos ". Le Prof. John Mc Murtry, membre de la Société royale du Canada voit un lien avec ce qu'il appelle *The Cancer Stage of Capitalism*, titre du livre où il écrit : "The trick of the endless US-led wars in the Middle East is to control both sides so as to ensure against sovereign states able to defend the common interests of their peoples" - cf. https://www.globalresearch.ca/planning-chaos-in-the-middle-east-destruction-of-societies-for-foreign-money-control/5445509. Voir aussi https://southfront.org/controlled-chaos-as-a-tool-of-geopolitical-struggle ou www.atimes.com/article/korea-afghanistan-never-ending-war-trap, et oumma.com/une-guerre-sans-fin-en-afghanistan. Etc.

Plunging countries into destruction, endless war and terror cannot be God's way. He does not need such plans. Every thinking believer will recognise here the work of Evil, who dreams of enslaving and destroying the world through a single power, which in Christian and Islamic traditions is precisely called the *Antichrist*.

Moreover, even without naming things, many non-believers also denounce these projects, which are sometimes incoherent and groping, but very real: certainly, there has never been *a* single plan at work, but certainly various wills caressing this or that project of world domination. In their time, what else did the Caliphs dream of?

Any plan to divide humanity in two and use one side against the other is contrary to the "right path" that not only individuals but also families and nations should follow. But how to get out of such a trap?

Becoming aware of the manipulations we are undergoing is a first step. But isn't the most decisive step to regain a *sense of the* right path, i.e. the expectation of the Day of God, which no man can anticipate or bring about in His place? A different and better world is possible, rationally and according to Christian traditions, but **after the Day of** Judgement and not **before**. To want to anticipate the Judgement, i.e. to start an "eschatological" war, is doubly senseless.

As you can see, the questions raised by this verse 6 of Fâtiḥah are immense.

7. An apposition against Jews and Christians

ṣirāṭa lladīna 'an'amta 'alayhim ġayri l-maġḍūbi 'alayhim wa-lā ḍ-ḍāllīna

the way of those whom Thou hast favoured, not of those who have incurred Thy wrath, nor of those who have gone astray

The last verse of Fâtiḥah is a long (*badal*) apposition to the word "path".

A consistent and unique tradition of commentary indicates that "those whom You have showered with favours" are Muslims, that "those who have incurred Your wrath" are Jews, and that "the lost" are Christians. The unanimity of this interpretation can be explained by the simple fact that these expressions refer to two passages of Sura 5 where, indeed, on the one hand the Jews are said to incur the wrath of God and on the other hand the Christians are said to be lost[5].

---

[5] Sura 5 *al-mā'ida* provides the two verses necessary for identification: verse 60 refers to the Jews "whom God has cursed, against whom He is angry" (Q 5:60); and following verses 72 and 73, which are clearly aimed at Christians, verse 77 states that they are "people who have already gone astray, who have gone astray many and who are going astray (with 3 times the verb *ḍallala*, Q 5:77)". If not from God, where do these hateful statements come from?

This question makes sense. It so happens that both anti-Jewish and anti-Christian sectarian groups preceded Islam, and precisely in areas

Also, it is not possible for a Jew or a Christian to recite Fâtiḥah: he would be condemning himself by saying this verse 7. But without this surprisingly long final verse, it could be said by any believer. It is recited every day and on every occasion by Muslims, who therefore, even if they do not think about it, constantly condemn Jews and Christians.

In fact, this final verse is really curious. Its apposition process is almost unique in the Qur'an, and this apposition is strangely long - much longer than any other verse. For various reasons (rhythm, structure, bad syntax, implicit reference to another sura...), many exegetes have thought that this verse 7 must have been added after the fact under the authority of a Caliph, perhaps when this so-called "opening" prayer (this is the meaning of the word fâtiḥah) was placed at the head of the Koran (although it is almost the shortest and should therefore be at the end).

Since then, this verse has tended to cut humanity in two - non-believers being assimilated into the "Christian world" according to Islamic discourse, and Hindus and other religious groups not even deserving of consideration. One Caliph skillfully used the most prayed sura in Islam. As we have seen, the thought of George

---

where many recent Islamological studies suggest that it actually originated. But this is another debate.

Bush dividing the world into "axis of Good" and "axis of Evil" is not very different.

It's a real shame that this verse was added, because Fâtiḥah could have been a beautiful prayer that everyone could have said.

II - Reflecting on the past and the future

Most of the work has been to ask the right questions, through Fâtiḥah, and to start addressing them. The journey must continue towards future prospects.

To do this, it is necessary to look more carefully at what is called "Judgement". The term "Antichrist", which is a person and, according to many Islamic traditions, one-eyed moreover, has been mentioned several times before. The Antichrist must close the present time since he must be judged and eliminated at Judgement. What can this mean?

1. Facing Judgment and the Antichrist

If we believe that God will condemn the camp of those who do evil, when will He do it, that is to say, when might "two camps" exist one day?

Two "camps" not discernible a priori

"A God who intervenes against the camp of evil": at first glance, and after the first part of this book, such a perspective seems unusual and unfounded. Yet it is part of the faith (biblical or Muslim). The innate sense of justice also gives it hope.

In reality, what is unfounded is the monstrous pretension of sorting in God's place, not the fact that God himself does it: it seems logical that one day all humans on earth will be forced to take a stand for or against God. Or more exactly against or for the Antichrist. The reason for this is quite simple. Let us suppose that one day a single Mafia power will be established over the world. Whoever would be at the head of it would no longer have a competitor and would not fail to show himself, being worshipped by all men - this is even what we have already seen, on a smaller scale, on the part of many totalitarian powers that claim a different essence from mortals, therefore almost divine.

In doing so, this unique Mafia leader, called *Antichrist* by those who do not love him (others will praise him), will have achieved the separation of humanity into two "camps". This separation will be due to him and will allow the Day of Judgement to come - this would even be the only "positive" aspect of this being of Evil, which helps to conceive why a God who does not want evil would let it manifest itself to the whole world.

Logically, one can understand better then that those who dream of dividing the world in two and subduing the "others" (the word *islâm* precisely means *submission*) are preparing and doing the work of the Antichrist precisely.

And certainly not God's.

Precedents in the history of Europe too

"In Europe, we have seen such projects, for example with atheistic communism, to which historians attribute one hundred million deaths: it separated humanity into two camps, the "socialist world" and the "world to be conquered". The English communist George Orwell came to take part in the Spanish Civil War (1936-1939) and, seeing the atrocities that the (socialist) ideology of salvation was causing on the "republican" side, he returned to England in disgust; he then wrote his novel "1984", in [6] which he denounced in advance the post-communist projects that would purify the earth and establish the perfect society.

Of course, similar ideas had already caused bloodshed in Europe, especially in the 15th century in the Czech Republic, when the Hussites took up arms against all those they considered to be... the henchmen of the Antichrist (just think about it!). A century later, Luther accused the pope of being the Antichris[7], which in turn triggered so-called "wars of religion". However, William Cavanaugh and others have shown that these were far more wars of seizure of power by sectarian groups using religious faith to deceive and entice people. Indeed, later revolutions and wars no longer tried to use the Bible to justify even worse sectarianism, they were even openly anti-Christian.

---

[6] After a first book in fable form, *Animals farm,* devoted to denouncing communism.

[7] Luther, *Complete Works* (*W.A.*), vol. 6, pp. 464, 12-157.

It should be noted here that the Gospel does not teach sectarianism on "both sides"; it is no doubt thanks to its latent influence that, despite everything, Europe overall remains a region of peace where people from all over the world seek refuge - which is not the case in any Muslim country. But this influence does not make this continent a collection of "Christian countries" as Islamist discourses and even those of the Turkish President, which are reminiscent of the communist discourses separating the world into capitalist or socialist countries, say. This is all the more delusional because, in European countries, and especially in those in the West which have known communism only in terms of ideology and dreams, Christian references are being increasingly discarded; all that remains of them is a vague consensus around the precept: "Do not do to others what you would not want them to do to you". Is this what disturbs Erdogan? In any case, in most of the Eastern countries (including Russia), which have had to mourn millions of deaths as a result of the totalitarian communist system, people's minds are today less closed to the influence of the Gospel.

These remarks may help to unblock minds which, especially from Europe, see the world divided into two "domains", the *dar al-islâm",* the world they fantasise about, and the *"dar al-ḥarb",* the depraved Christian world to be conquered (literally: "of war"). This Islamist mental schema is widespread.

A psychiatric approach will never be able to overcome such a mental pattern. It is linked to a religious type of logic and also to the very meaning of the words: *Muslims* mean *submitted to* God (and therefore promised to Heaven), which implies that the *rebels* constitute "the other side" (and that they are doomed to Hell, whatever they do). Terrible Islamist logic of words and ideas.

Nothing can shake this logic, except by showing that it is held precisely by those who are preparing the Antichrist and already working for him.

A world that respects everyone?

We will not be content to denounce: we can also open up a positive perspective, even if it is not completely for today: in the logic of the coming Judgement, it is normal that the achievements are for *afterwards*. In the logic of the coming Judgement, it is normal that the accomplishments are for afterwards. The very fact of hoping for them for *afterwards is the* foundation of what is most positive and most beautiful for society. What does this mean? A tale allows us to say simply with images what is a little difficult to grasp abstractly[8] .

Once upon a time there was a rich peasant whose fields were coveted by an agro-food multinational (which we will not name). After sowing promising traditional seeds in his fields, the multinational discreetly planted his own

---

[8] A parallel story can be found in Mt 13, 13-30 + 36-43.

GMO (genetically modified organism) seeds by plane to contaminate his fields and then get him into trouble and ruin him in endless lawsuits. The peasant had hired unemployed jihadists to guard his fields, and they later realised the danger. They came to the boss and told him: "Tomorrow we have to call José Bové and mow down all the GMO sprouts; we're going to eradicate the evil". He replied, "No, don't do any of that, you risk cutting the good shoots with the others. When they are all ripe, I will bring Mr. Bové who will guide the specialised harvesters, and they will be able to cut and destroy the GMOs without damaging the good plants, and we will have a good harvest".

Then he added: "All this should make you think about what will happen on Judgment Day. The "good" ones are like the traditional seeds that grow among GMOs, but they can't know who the "bad" ones are. Those who study the population - sociologists and psychologists - cannot know that either, let alone politicians, who should start by looking at themselves. So who will be the specialised harvesters who will help God to sort out on Judgement Day? They will not be men, but angels; under the guidance of the Christ who will have come, they will throw all the wicked with the Antichrist into Hell. No man can do this, and certainly not now".

This tale in the form of a parable makes sense. If the Judgement is to come, it can only be realised on the Day of the Harvest and certainly not by the work of men. And the key to respect for others lies in waiting for this Day: no one has the right to anticipate it and therefore to consider others as evil - to be eradicated or "subdued".

"Tolerance" or respect?

Thus, such a parable founds what is called "tolerance" - there is no other possible foundation against Islamism and other messianisms. Nevertheless, let us be careful with words. The word *tolerance is* often used instead of *respect, but* not without a double danger.

First of all, it is an evil that we "tolerate". Even Islamists say they are tolerant, in the sense that they tolerate cockroaches in their homes that they are unable to kill for the moment: they say they tolerate the *kafir-s (*or *miscreants*) in the sense that they will not kill them as long as they pay them the *dzijyah,* which is a kind of right to live. But what is such "tolerance", if not a form of "neantisation of the other", as Claude Lévi-Strauss used to say, or of "hate crime" as we say today?

The other danger of the word "tolerance" is its use by anti-Muslim libertarians: they say that one must be "tolerant" of all current ways of life, especially "sexual" ones, as if it were a lack of respect for people to have another opinion. It is a danger of serious and hypocritical confusion between people, who deserve respect, and acts that do not deserve it. This confusion greatly paralyses the defence of those who are the victims - especially children, who are sacrificed to this ideology.

43

It is important to use the right words.

Knowing how to listen rationally

It is equally important to take seriously Muslim traditions that speak of the Antichrist, even if some aspects seem delusional - at least they speak of it much more often than the current Christian discourse. Western rationalist thought is easily reticent about these traditions, especially the idea of a "Messiah Jesus" (as the Koran says) coming down from heaven to earth to kill the antichrist dragon, to lead a worldwide army battle, and to live there for another forty years (or until the age of forty, depending on the version).

However, the Christian version (which is original) is simpler. It evokes a manifestation of Jesus "on the clouds". Such a vision, imposed on all, is sufficient to explain the Judgement. It is true that Christian traditions are not as prolific on the *how of* the Judgement as those of Islam (which become obscure and contradictory); but modern psychology undoubtedly brings some light here: when faced with absolute evidence that one cannot escape, it seems that the human mind cannot deny it without incurring serious, perhaps fatal, damage. In any case, the question is open. And, like those of Islam, these traditions speak of a continuation (until Christ "hands over his kingdom to the Father"[9]).

---

[9] 1Co 15, 22-28. According to 2Th 2:3-12, the Antichrist will be annihilated while the righteous will be enlivened (Heb 9:28).

Human beings live according to the representations they make of the future - that of their life on earth (personal or community) and that of the Beyond. It would be completely irrational not to take this into account. This is, however, what has been done in terms of 'deradicalisation', insofar as we have neither understood nor even listened to Islamist logic. This very closed logic, giving pride of place to what is called "eschatology", seems to be concrete. But it can be turned around more easily than we think. On condition that you enter into the thought of the other, Islamist thought.

2. Foundations of civil agreement?

What can we really hope for? We can't be content with an absence of perspective that would lead to nihilism, nor with a consumerist culture that promises to have everything and everything right away and that holds out the promise of a "living together" that would be nothing more than a utopia.

Currently undermined by a massive influx of migrants, integration has worked despite the fact that communitarianism has been and is still being promoted. The *Strasbourg Resolutions of* 7 and 8 June 1975 explicitly requested that "immigrants also have the right to export

---

Irenaeus, a disciple of a disciple of the apostle John, raises these questions in his treatise *Against Heresies*. Cf. Fr. Breynaert, *The Glorious Coming of Christ,* Paris, Jubilee 2016.

their culture to Europe, to propagate and disseminate it.... "»[10] .

However, our reflections on Fâtiḥah suggest that it is possible to envisage a more efficient and more faith-based integration of the Muslim community:

✓   This integration should involve working across community divides in the face of very real general threats (which the Muslim community as a whole perceives in relation to the Antichrist).

✓   This integration could involve sharing the hope of a better world on this earth, provided that it is situated, as seen by believers, in a world beyond the "day of judgement".

For all of this, we need to get rid of suprematism and victimisation.

Breaking away from suprematism

Suprematism is both an inner and outer attitude based on the conviction of belonging to a human group superior to the rest of humanity. This Islamist identity can be based

---

[10] See Eurabia No. 2 published by the European Coordinating Committee for Friendship with the Arab World, cf. http://nageltjes.be/wp/wp-content/uploads/2014/04/Tekst-Resolutie-van-Straatsburg-8-juni-1975.pdf. These surprising documents make it possible to understand why, as early as 1976, laws were passed for "family reunification", and others later on that favoured and exacerbated communitarianism.

on the Koranic formula: "You are the best community that has ever arisen for mankind" (3, 110). The idea of "chosen people" comes from the Bible, but this holy text never describes a superiority that would have been devolved to Judaism, but a mission of witness and holiness in the midst of other men.

It was for this purpose that a system of "separate kitchen" and "pure and unclean" was established: according to the apostle Paul, a specialist in Jewish law, this system of separation followed only pedagogical objectives (cultic and cultural, cf. Galatians 3:24); it was never to be used to put in the minds of children that they are superior to the rest of humanity. Moreover, he says again, these objectives are outdated.

Today, especially in Europe, the practice of Halal is generally a way of expressing one's "difference" in the sense of a supremacist setting aside others as "impure". This practice, which was not practised in Europe by the first generations of immigrants, should have been banned: it feeds sectarianism. On the contrary, the public authorities have knowingly encouraged it and continue to do so...

A few remarks are therefore in order:

- A God who means no harm charges no one to crush others, be it non-Muslims, women or other Muslims (the issue of slavery is very real, it is regularly defended by

Salafist preachers, and there are even fatwas to justify enslaving Muslims - theoretically forbidden in Islam).

- But a God who has only a relationship of *domination/submission* with mankind puts a terrible burden on human relations, which can hardly escape this model.

- As for personal conscience, the pressure of the "Ummah" tends to diminish it, so that only the opinion of the group - especially among Islamists - counts. However, one cannot progress, in faith as in life, without a certain personal and moral conscience, which will say: "I am responsible" - the word "I" being as important as "responsible". There is no future for society as a whole without collaboration between people capable of saying and thinking "I".

It will take time to get out of these mental confinements. However, it should be remembered that no journey can be made without the initial impulse, which is linked to a reversal of "eschatology", that is to say, essentially, of the notion of Judgement.

As an opening to new perspectives, we can cite Paul's formula, which sheds light on all healthy secularism (and the notion of equality):

"From now on, there is neither Jew nor Greek (= non-Jew), there is neither slave nor free man, male nor female" (Galatians 3:28).

Of course, such a strong formula must be read throughout Paul's teaching: it does not mean that there would be no more differences or order in creation. Nor does it call into question legitimate differences or preferences, by virtue of family ties for example: it is normal and legitimate that we think first of all about helping our loved ones rather than others. It is the ideological deviation of the notion of equality that makes us say that everyone should be treated the same, which would be radically unfair. What Paul vigorously denounces as illegitimate is discrimination based on (supposed) superiority in the context of supremacist systems of domination:

- supremacist religious domination (some would have been chosen above the others by God);
- Slavery, which consists of denying any right to human groups;
- the enslavement of women, as if relations between men and women were solely a question of sex and reproduction (hence the rather crude terms used by Paul).

It will be noted that it is precisely these three dominations that Islamist preachers teach.

Moreover, in one way or another, they always go together, there are links. It is men more than women who dream of supremacist world domination projects, and it is usually women who want to turn men (wives and mothers) away from them. This is why suprematist thinking tends to prevent them from existing socially (at least as women), to the point of forcing them to hide their faces. There can be no 'living together' if women do not have the right to exist (and as women!).

Identity-based supremacist convictions are not reserved for Islamists. All organisations aiming at domination and submission will persuade their members that they are part of superior beings, and even that others are not really men. This also applies to nations founded on such a spirit. When one hears: "America remains the only indispensable nation in the world" (William J. Clinton, *Inaugural Address,* January 20, 1997)[11], one is almost as worried as when one hears the speeches of Wahhabi preachers.

Getting rid of "victimisation".

The rejection of any spirit of suprematism will be the fruit of patient work. But this is not the only psychological trait linked to Islamist mental confinement: there is also "victimisation". The idea of posing as a victim, especially communally, can be understood in relation to the guilt of a target public: the aim is to establish psychological domination over it and, of course, to extort advantages from it. The former sixty-eight former Freudo-Marxists have become masters in this art, from which they benefit

---

[11] Or again: "The United States has been and will remain the only indispensable nation in world affairs" (Barack Obama, *Speech to the National Veterans Convention,* Reno, 23 July 2012). Etc.

various groups (real or fantasised) by creating new social "sins".

In these games of psychological, media and legal manipulation, Islamists occupy a nice niche with the notion of "Islamophobia". It functions at the same time as an accusatory and identity-based discourse. Such victimizing propaganda finds favourable ground among young people who only know their host country through their community and who feel frustrated by the goods they see on television; but it also finds some elsewhere. If 'Islamophobia' is a disease, as the word suggests, it does not affect non-Muslim circles: it is a phobia of Islamists who imagine themselves to be victims of the non-Muslim world. It is a disease in the sense that it disrupts any correct social perception and, of course, makes human relations (e.g. at work) difficult. This reinforces victimisation: the Islamist is a victim by nature, he is innocent and unjustly 'discriminated against', he must take revenge because, as innocent, he can restore justice.

Even more than suprematism, this disease has a religious dimension. For the idea of innocence by which justice is to be restored is biblical, and it is above all Christian. This is not easy to understand.

In 2004-2005, the film 'The Passion of the Christ' (2004) was more successful among Muslims and as far away as Saudi Arabia (where people watched it on pirated DVDs), than with Western audiences. A reaction at the time says it all : " Palestinians are still subjected to the same kind of

51

suffering that Jesus suffered during the crucifixion "[12]. Such an assimilation seems confusing because, in Islamic logic, an envoy of God can only be victorious, and the film shows a crucified envoy of God ! Fortunately, the film ends with the resurrection - so, in fact, Jesus is finally victorious. But it is something else that has touched the Islamic audience so much: the dimension of Judgement is strongly emphasised in the film. And the bloodshed.

Indeed, we see Satan-Iblis, very much personified in the film, losing his power because of the shed blood of the total innocent who offers his life. However, the blood shed is that of the sheep during Eid al-Kebir, which represents the sacrifice of the son of Abraham (it doesn't matter which son), which did not take place. It is also that of the "rebels" that the Islamists slaughter. It is also that of the "martyr" (*shayd*) who loses his life after trying to kill as many of God's enemies as possible. Jesus did not kill anyone. This is a knot that deserves to be looked at when talking to Islamists.

Karpman's observations are obviously true here: whoever poses as a victim easily turns into an executioner - or a saviour. Victimisation is a complex manipulation that gives meaning to the lives of community members. This meaning goes far beyond communalist claims and the benefits that are hoped for: it is the conviction of

---

[12] Nabil Abu Rudeina, Official Information Service of the Palestinian National Authority, 21 March 2004.

participating in the restoration of Justice, that is, in Judgement.

This is why it will not be possible to help to get out of such irrational and complex victimized mentalities without tackling the question of the Day of Judgement, which precisely the jihadists believe they are anticipating. By this means, we can get out of it.

Agreeing on the rejection of evil and the "common good".

Finally, we will be able to show the convergences between people concerned about the good and the future. What generally drives diverse people to unite is a danger that threatens them together. We can think that we are in this case facing a global threat that is similar to that of the Antichrist.

Today, there is no shortage of threats to our children's future. All of them are linked to suprematisms, that is to say, to systems of thought and power that give themselves rights over the good of others, over their children, over their minds, etc. This is the case of Islamism which, in its form of jihad, is widely used in the world to "dialectise" civil societies: to drown the more or less Islamised populations in order to oppose them to the rest of the population - including through war - and thus plunge peoples and nations into a "controlled chaos" in order to make them dependent and enslaved. This also happens in 'Muslim' countries: let us never forget the two hundred thousand deaths of the Algerian Islamist war (between 1990 and 1998).

The logic of the rediscovery of a certain "common good" (a notion incomprehensible a priori by Islamists) passes through the rejection of all suprematisms, and therefore through the rejection of the use of one against the other, according to the game wanted by those who work to lock the world into a dialectic (be this or that, but choose your side!). The one who divides, the "dialectician", is called in Greek *diabolos* - i.e. Satan-Iblis. Are we going to continue working in the service of such chaos?

Conclusion

The 'deradicalisation' proposed here is, by its very nature, much broader than a simple 'method'. We have even been led to reflect on the meaning and possibility of a better world! We must go so far as to close the door to the dreadful reveries that claim to sort men between good and bad, and decide which ones deserve to live and which ones should disappear.

In terms of de-radicalisation, it is now recognised that government initiatives have not borne the hoped-for fruits, and even that the failure is total. Undoubtedly, the fundamental fault lies in having wanted to treat radical Islamist belief as a psychological or sociological phenomenon. On the contrary, we have shown that it was necessary to enter into its very object, and that it is possible and necessary to rationally approach Islamist desire and hope, even and especially with the most fanatical: to ignore a belief that has such deep roots was senseless and irrational.

And we have seen that, if a reign of God is to come, it is certainly not imposable: it can only be prepared, by those who walk a straight path, the path of those who fight all suprematism and who are open to the Common Good.

Foreword... 3

Introduction 5

I - Asking the problems: read Sura Al Fâtiḥah 9

1. Allah-God and Mercy...9
   The word "Allah"..10
   Both terms raḥmān and raḥīm....................................10
2. Desire for the "God of the universe".......................13
3. An emphasis on God's mercy 16
4. A Judgement to come..18
   The words...18
   Who will judge who and how?......................................19
5. To worship and implore God? 23
6. The right path 25
   The pre-Islamic doctrine of the "two ways". 25
   Bad means but good end? 28
   Trap and handling 30
7. An apposition against Jews and Christians 34

II - Reflecting on the past and the future 37

1. Facing Judgment and the Antichrist.......................37
   Two "camps" not discernible a priori............................37
   Precedents in the history of Europe too 38
   A world that respects everyone? 41
   "Tolerance" or respect? 43
   Knowing how to listen rationally 44
2. Foundations of civil agreement?............................45
   Breaking away from suprematism 46
   Getting rid of "victimisation". 50
   Agreeing on the rejection of evil and the "common good".
  53

Conclusion 55